TIME! LADIES AND GENTLEMEN:
A FEW THOUGHTS ON LAST THINGS

In response to James Sale's Trilogy: *HellWard*, *StairWell*, and *Doorway*

FRANCIS ETHEREDGE

Foreword by James Sale

EN ROUTE BOOKS AND MEDIA, LLC
SAINT LOUIS, MO

ENROUTE
Make the time

En Route Books and Media, LLC
5705 Rhodes Avenue
St. Louis, MO 63109

Cover art generated by Sebastian Mahfood
using ChatGPT

Copyright © 2025 Francis Etheredge

ISBN-13: 979-8-88870-486-8
Library of Congress Control Number:
Available online at https://catalog.loc.gov

No part of this book may be reproduced, stored in a retrieval system, or transmitted in any form, or by any means, electronic, mechanical, photocopying, or otherwise, without the prior written permission of the author.

Table of Contents

Foreword: Touched by a Tear by James Sale iii
    The Theological Mirror v
    The DoorWay of Glory vii
    A Communion of Poets viii
    The Judgment that is Mercy x
    The Wider Circle xi

Introduction: Ignorance of Christ is Ignorance of Self ... 1
    Three kinds of published work 3
    My Words Bled 6

Chapter One: "Read! Repent! And Rejoice!": A Reflection on James Sale's Modernization of Dante's *Inferno* 15
    Introduction: Pope Francis and James Sale 16
    Christ, Sale himself, and Dante 17
    Dante as companion 20
    In Conclusion 23

"HELL'S-HOLE: AN UNBIDDEN MERCY": PROSE AND POEM PRAYER 25

Chapter Two: Jesus said to Him: "Get Up, Pick Up Your Mat and Walk" (John 5: 8): A Reflection on James Sale's *StairWell* 31

Introduction: When Change is a Gift of God 31

Where to go from here? To go back in order to go forward! 34

Hell and suffering: Purgatory and Suffering 42

"OH MOTHER OF THE STAIRS": PROSE AND POEM-PRAYER 49

Chapter Three: "DoorWay" to 'The Lord of All': A Reflection on James Sale's *DoorWay* 59

Introduction: Why the theme of the 'butterfly'? 60

Part I: Retracing my steps: HellWard and StairWell 64

Part II: A Theological Reflection and a Poet's Intuition 69

Part III: The Poignancy of the Butterfly 71

In Conclusion 77

"INDELIBLE": PROSE AND POEM PRAYER 79

Conclusion: His Judgement is Mercy 93

Foreword: Touched by a Tear
by James Sale

It is a strange and moving thing to see one's own imaginative work refracted through the mind and heart of another — stranger still when that other is a man of such conviction, faith, and theological integrity as Francis Etheredge. I began my *English Cantos* — *HellWard*, *StairWell*, and *DoorWay* — as a modern re-imagining of Dante's *Divine Comedy*: not a translation, not even an imitation, but a spiritual continuation, written in the idiom of our age and out of my own experience of near death, love, and loss. But what Francis has done in this remarkable little volume is to take that poetic journey and infuse it with his own pilgrimage — a life steeped in prayer, suffering, and the ardent pursuit of Christ. His *Commentary on a Trilogy* is no mere review or critical appreciation; it is, in its way, a conversion narrative, a confession of faith set alight by another's words.

I am reminded that all genuine art, if it truly seeks truth, opens a door that others may walk through. The artist may not know who will follow, or how far they will go, yet his task is to make the opening. Francis has walked through the door I opened and has found there a chamber of his own — filled with Scripture, theology, and the unmistakable fragrance of grace. He has, in effect, written not about my trilogy, but through it, using its poetic architecture as scaffolding for his own ascent toward self-knowledge and divine encounter. It is therefore profoundly fitting that the opening section of his book bears the title "Ignorance of Christ is Ignorance of Self."

Francis adapts St Jerome's axiom — that ignorance of Scripture is ignorance of Christ — and turns it, deftly, toward the interior life. For him, and I believe for all of us, to know Christ is to begin to know oneself truly; to reject Him is to wander in a fog of half-perceptions. His book is thus an act of illumination, seeking in poetry the same revelatory power that theology seeks in doctrine. That, of course, is also Dante's purpose; and if I have attempted, in my own *Cantos*, to show the modern soul's journey from despair through repentance to illumination, Francis has in turn traced that journey within himself, finding that every descent is a call to mercy and every ascent a gift of grace.

The Theological Mirror

In *HellWard*, Francis perceives what he calls "a message of mercy" — that even the contemplation of hell is meant to save us from it. He quotes my own observation that "it's not so much that God puts us there, but that we end up where we want to be", and he recognises, with that clear-eyed compassion of the theologian, that the true horror of damnation is the human will turned irrevocably inward. Yet he does not linger in horror; he sees, through the infernal imagery, the light that still glimmers. He invokes Dante's phrase, "the ample arms of God", to remind us that even in the poem's darkest scenes, there remains the outstretched mercy of the Father waiting to receive the penitent.

That, I think, is Francis's greatest gift as a reader: he never mistakes the depiction of sin for an endorsement of it, nor the darkness of the journey for the absence of God. He understands that art can speak of evil precisely in order to awaken the longing for good. His commentary on *HellWard* is therefore a homily on freedom — the dreadful freedom to choose hell, and the redemptive freedom to cry out for salvation. When he describes my mother's figure in the poem — that tragic emblem of the soul clinging to its own bondage — he reads it as a universal allegory of the will that will not yield. He writes with the candour of one who has wrestled with the same angel and bears the same wound.

From this descent, he ascends, as Dante and I both sought to do, toward purification. *StairWell* becomes, in his hands, a meditation on forgiveness, centred on the reconciliation between mother and son. His theological reading turns this scene — which for me was always both intimate and metaphysical — into a vision of purgatory as love's surgery: the painful stripping away of self-deception until the soul, purified of its own poison, can breathe again. Francis reads the episode with a profound empathy born of his own history — a life marked by loss, by the long road back to the Church, and by a chastened joy in marriage and fatherhood. For him, the stairwell is not merely an image of ascent; it is the gradual return of trust, the rediscovery that suffering, accepted, becomes participation in the Cross.

He weaves into this reflection the wisdom of saints and philosophers — St Thomas Aquinas, C. S.

Lewis, Helen Roseveare — but always with the humility of one who speaks from experience, not authority. When he writes, citing Roseveare, that "God never uses a person greatly until He has wounded him deeply," he speaks for all who have found in affliction the strange anointing of purpose. His own prose-poem "Oh Mother of the Stairs" stands as a prayer for prisoners, outcasts, and all who dwell, literally or spiritually, in confinement. It reminds us that even within the prison cell, one can begin the ascent toward the light.

The DoorWay of Glory

Finally, in *DoorWay*, Francis discovers the symbol that binds the whole together — the butterfly. It is a delicate yet potent emblem: the metamorphosis of death into life, of loss into transfiguration. He notes that for me the butterfly is personal — the image of a child lost to abortion — and he treats that revelation not as a biographical curiosity but as a theological key. In the butterfly's fragile wings he perceives the mystery of resurrection: the soul released from the chrysalis of corruption, rising into colour and freedom. He relates this to the Church's reflection on unbaptised infants, discerning in the mercy of God a hope that surpasses all law.

For Francis, heaven is not abstract radiance but the flowering of every sorrow into meaning. He quotes my lines on baptism as a stripping away of the "body's deadening crepe", seeing in them the enactment of what theology calls sanctification — that lifelong shedding of sin which ends, finally, in glory. Here his own voice becomes one of doxology: he praises not the poet but the divine artistry that turns even our words, our wounds, into instruments of grace.

A Communion of Poets

What moves me most in reading *Commentary on a Trilogy* is the sense of companionship it evokes. Dante, I wrote, was given Virgil as his guide through Hell and Purgatory; I, in writing, often felt Dante himself beside me; and now Francis has joined that company, walking a few paces behind yet singing in harmony. His commentary does not compete with mine; it completes it, revealing dimensions I had only partially intuited. He sees what I felt but could not name — that poetry and theology, when true, are twin disciplines of revelation.

In that sense, Francis Etheredge is not merely a commentator but a fellow pilgrim. He too has descended into the shadowlands of despair and ascended, bruised but believing, into the daylight of mercy. His autobiographical passages — the basement conversion, the rediscovered vocation, the life of prayer with his large family — give flesh to the abstractions of grace. They remind us that redemption is not a metaphor but a reality unfolding in time, that the Gospel is not an idea but an event lived anew in every soul that says "Yes."

And because he is a Catholic writer — deeply so, though never narrowly — his work breathes the universality of that vision. He draws freely on Scripture, the Fathers, and the Magisterium, yet his tone is never sectarian. Indeed, as one who now worships within the Anglican tradition, I find in his pages nothing alien but much that unites: a shared reverence for the Word, a shared sense of the sacraments as channels of grace, a shared belief that art itself can be a mode of praise. We differ in churchmanship, perhaps, but not in aspiration; we both seek the Light that lighteth every man who cometh into the world.

The Judgment that is Mercy

The closing words of his book — "His Judgement is Mercy" — could serve as an epitaph for all our striving. They express that paradox at the heart of Dante's vision, and of mine: that divine justice is not retribution but restoration, that love itself is the refining fire. Francis understands this not as an abstract principle but as the lived reality of faith. In his own sufferings — physical, psychological, spiritual — he has found what the saints found: that the wounds of Christ are the doors of healing.

In this he stands in the great tradition of English religious writers — those who unite personal experience with theological insight: Julian of Norwich, George Herbert, T. S. Eliot. Like them, he writes not to display knowledge but to bear witness. His prose has the cadence of prayer; his poems bleed, to use his own phrase, yet the blood is life. To read him after reading my own *Cantos* is to see the same mountain from another side — the same ascent, but through different weather, different terrain.

The Wider Circle

For readers approaching this volume, I would say: do not treat it as criticism but as companion. Let it read you as much as you read it. Francis Etheredge has undertaken here a task both humble and heroic: to follow another's poem into the depths of theology and to emerge with a bouquet of mercy. His work reminds us that poetry is not escape but encounter — an opening of the intellect and imagination to the divine Word that still speaks through human words. Ideally, this work complements *The English Cantos*.

It gives me immense joy to commend this book to you. It testifies that the dialogue between poet and reader can itself become sacramental: the word received, pondered, and given back transfigured. If my *English Cantos* were meant as a journey from hell through purgatory to paradise, then Francis's *Commentary* is the echo of that journey in another soul — proof that the Word does not return void.

May every reader who opens these pages hear, through the voices of two poets and the whisper of the Spirit between them, that same invitation Dante heard and I have tried to renew: to turn, to rise, to enter at last through the Doorway of the Lord of All.

Introduction

Ignorance of Christ is Ignorance of Self

We do not always know the outcome of a piece of work or whether it will be a standalone article, a short book, or a longer work; and, indeed, what combination of pieces may make a whole.

So, it was with this short book as, to begin with, I wrote to a poet, James Sale, asking for a poem to go in a book of mine[1]; and then, as the poet was working on a modern version of Dante's trilogy: Inferno; Purgatorio; and Paradiso, I was drawn to respond to the first book, then the second and, finally, the third: *HellWard; StairWell*; and *DoorWay*. Although serious, technically serious poetry, is not my strength, still the power of imagery, coupled with psychological and spiritual sufferings, are not foreign to me personally or to the times in which we live. However, very often, our sufferings are medicalised, rather than analysed or enlightened by the word of God.

---

[1] James Sale, "Could I But", in *Honest Rust and Gold: A Second Collection of Prose and Poetry*: https://enroutebooksandmedia.com/ honestrustandgold/.

Therefore my response has been through the theological study which has characterised many years of my life and, in a particular way, has filled to overflowing the last ten years or so. At the same time, this theological study has been accompanied by a study of the Word of God; and, as such, is a word which constantly opens me up to myself and my God. Starting from St. Jerome's famous adage, "Ignorance of Scripture is ignorance of Christ", I have adapted it to continue along the vein of self-knowledge: "Ignorance of Christ is Ignorance of Self", although I have not put it like that before. This is because self-knowledge entails knowing Christ as indeed it entails recognising ourselves as sinners in need of a saviour.

Altogether, then, we arrive at this short book, which is a combination of my three response to the Sale's trilogy and the accrued work, as it were, which coalesces around these themes: self-knowledge and ignorance; hell; and heaven. And, as such, I begin with a piece which sums up the often-fruitless searching of many years, which included running away from the suffering entailed in writing, rewriting, pasting, cutting, Tipp-exing, for those who remember the white liquid we used to paint over our mistakes, sellotaping extra pages or patches until, desperate to escape the impossible treadmill of being unable finish my first books, I tried to abandon writing completely.

Following, then, an account of my published work, which is nothing short of miraculous, I take up the theme of a beginning: a kind of naturalistic account of self-knowledge. The body of work, however, is a gift of God in that with all the difficulties of life, health, working, studying, a late marriage and a family life with eight children, we both have no debts, even if we are not well off, with the writing coming together after years of false starts, occasional published pieces, and many courses which involved a lot of written work.

Three kinds of published work

The following titles are now on Amazon, in production or, as with this book, in the process of being written; but I list them here in three groups: Scripture, theology, and philosophy; Bioethics; and autobiographical works; indeed, the third group began with a prayer in front of the Lady Chapel at our local

Catholic Church, in the hope of writing a more widely accessible read.

Scripture: A Unique Word (2014); *A trilogy on Faith and Reason called, From Truth and truth: Volume I-Faithful Reason* (2016), *Volume II-Faith and Reason in Dialogue* (2016), *Volume III-Faith is Married Reason* (2016).

A second section of work, then, focuses on primarily bioethical questions. *The Human Person: A Bioethical Word* (2017); *Conception: An Icon of the Beginning* (2019); *Mary and Bioethics: An Exploration* (2020); *Reaching for the Resurrection: A Pastoral Bioethics* (2020); and *Unfolding a Post-Roe World* (2022); and *Human Nature: Moral Norm* (2023). Furthermore, the National Catholic Bioethics Centre of America invited a contribution to Volume Two of a book on *Human Embryo Adoption: Catholic Arguments for and against*; my contribution is called "The Annunciation and Embryo Adoption" and argues that embryo adoption is a Marian participation in the saving work of Jesus Christ (2025). While the following two books have autobiographical elements, as do most other books, they are more about the situation of our times than personal experience and, therefore, they warrant being in this section. *The Word in Your Heart: Mary, Youth, and Mental Health* (2024); *Transgenderism: A Question of Identity* (2025), which ranges over our society and comes to a gradual focus on transgenderism, which has turned up, little by little, in a previous book. Francis Etheredge, together with Elizabeth Rex, co-authored *The Zygote of Christ and the Mystery of Man* (2025). And also this one, *Transgenderism Two: Evidence and Identity* (2025), which examines more deeply the recent documentation from the Supreme Court of the United Kingdom, a Report on Paediatric Medicine from America, and a Family Court Judgement from Australia, along with other material. What then follows, in this section, is a summary book on the major work which has been published up to now in this collection, called *A Shorter Bioethics* (2025).

The third section of work is much more autobiographical and covers a variety of life events: *The Family on Pilgrimage: God Leads Through Dead Ends* (2018); *The Prayerful Kiss: A Collection of Poetry and Prose* (2019); *Honest Rust and Gold: A Second Collection of Prose and Poetry* (2020); *Within Reach of You: A Book of Prose and Prayers* (2021); and *Lord, Do You*

Mean Me? A father-Catechist! (2023), *An Unlikely Gardener: A Book of Prose and Poetry* (2023).

MY WORDS BLED

As I did, it is possible to have many religious experiences and yet to know nothing of myself or God. This is because we need more than to hear our name called, to see a line of Scripture cross the horizon of our consciousness, "What does it profit a man to obtain the whole world and to lose his own soul?"[2] while driving the motorways to make money as a portacabin maintenance man, or to have the experience of "smelling the despair of the damned" as a warning that if we do not believe in the mercy of God we will die in our sins[3] – we need a saturation with the word of God which then, like a hillside after a heavy rainfall, starts to spring streams of living water[4].

However, just as we begin where we are, so God acts in our history to bring about change; but change is accompanied by His word and His Church. In

---

[2] Mark 8: 36.
[3] John 8: 24.
[4] John 4: 14.

Introduction: Ignorance of Christ is Ignorance of Self

other words, it was after many years of listening to the word of God in the *Neocatechumenal Way* that my experience of suffering began to make sense in terms of sin and salvation. Nevertheless, this first piece arises out of that early period, which went on until I was forty, during which I was restless without realizing my life was a pilgrimage from self-ignorance to knowledge of Christ. But just as a pilgrimage has a concrete path, so does passing from ignorance to Christ: that path is the word of God, Christian fellowship, and the liturgies of the Catholic Church.

This first piece, then, written before I started studying theology and reading, and listening to the word of God, is called "My Words Bled"; and, in the drama of its opening words, is the distress of years of initial writing that seemed to spring from nowhere and grind down the writer into abandoning the spring from which they came. Discovering myself to be a writer did not come naturally; indeed, writing was one of many possibilities. I tried to become a footballer, a craftsman, a painter, a sculptor, a journeyman maintenance man, a philosopher, a musician and many other things. In a certain sense, then, many failures made possible the success of succeeding to continue to write.

In the process of becoming a writer, one who writes, there is beginning to emerge more of a definition to being a writer: of being a kind of anthropological explorer. Beginning with my own experience, writing is like finding that the psychological, philosophical and theological dimensions of human existence are expanding "shells": a kind of fluidly moving "energy of meaning" that seems to be one place and, at the same time, touches "all" other places. The words of this poem, then, reflect on that initial bleeding; but bleeding, if unchecked, leads to death: the death of a writer. Nevertheless, this was a beginning.

My Words Bled

Like a too fruitful sapling: unstoppable.
I wrote too much and exhausted
the body of the spring in which they ran.

I fled like a snail from its shell.
Prematurely leaving home, I neither left it nor could
rest in it;

and not inhabiting its purpose made me homeless:
a disordered upgrowing in an ingrowing unhappi-
ness.

Like a surgeon operating on his own stomach -
but not a surgeon nor with a scalpel -
only a loose mirror and a home-made knife.

I fell underground.
Lying in the silence, desperate to do nothing;
doing nothing I did what nothing can do:
listening in the damp muddy warmth
and breathing in the sight of a shepherd's lamp.

I visited myself in the company of others
and suffered their incision.
I wrote again:
far fewer words fell
like footsteps in the autumn;
or the first winged leaves
of an acorn
outbreaking a scabby compost[5]

---

[5] From Part V of "The Prayerful Kiss": https://enroute-booksand media.com/theprayerfulkiss/

And so, after many years of being called back to the Catholic Church, I have now ceased going in and out like I did, through a revolving door, and I am gradually making sense of my life because of it. The founding experience, as it were, which itself constituted a change of heart was completely unexpected.

After many years of intermittently living away from home, whether completely inaccessibly, owing to no mobile phones, or just from time to time, I would return from time to time. This time, just before becoming 40, I had returned home and was living in the basement flat of my parent's house; and, after yet another failed relationship, I was sitting alone. There were three possibilities: more sin; madness; and suicide. However, for the last five years I had been studying theology and, whether it was for an essay or for some other reason, I was reading the *Catechism of the Catholic Church*. The Catechism said: that if God can create everything out of nothing He can create a new beginning for the sinner (CCC, 298); and, without anyone speaking, without any commentary, without explanation, I believed what I read, recognized myself as that sinner, God as my saviour, and I went back to the Catholic Church.

I was invited to go on a pilgrimage and I was given a random Gospel, one chosen by God not by me or anyone else; and it was the Gospel of the woman caught in adultery to whom Christ says: "Go and sin no more" (John 8: 11). Thus, it was that at 40, after many years of failed relationships, that the Lord was abundantly merciful and, literally, changed my life. After about a year, discovering that I was not called to the priesthood, my fiancé and I went to see our parish priest, Fr. Tony Trafford, who asked me to get a job. I was asked to get a job when I was discerning the possibility of becoming a priest and I just carried on writing poetry and earning a pound a piece.

Again I was asked to get a job and, according to Fr. Tony, I was at work in a laundry that same day, earning 3. 50 pence an hour in a place so hot that when I went for a Guinness one day, I drank two pints without it even touching the sides of my throat. Secondly, our courtship was chaste and, except very occasionally, and only with the slightest touch of the lips, we scarcely kissed. We also read the book of Tobit from beginning to end and took from it, in our marriage of nearly thirty years, to pray whenever we come together as husband and wife (cf. Tobit 8: 4-8).

So, like Sarah and Tobias, we came from the same religious family, as it were, the *Neocatechumenal Way*, and married. Furthermore, on the morning of marrying, I was outside my basement flat, looking at the beautiful October, sun-lit morning, when the words of the psalm ran through my mind: 'This poor man called and the Lord heard him' (Psalm 34: 6). We married and, as I say, we have now both been married and even renewed our marriage vows in Cana, in Galilee, where Mary, the mother of Jesus Christ, said to her son that the wine ran out (cf. John 2: 1-12). And, so, this word has stayed with us throughout our married life and always been an encouragement during difficult times.

But, more widely, the word of God continues to deepen my understanding of what God has done for me. Thus, the words at the end of Psalm 94 (95), sum up my life:

> For forty years that generation repelled me,
> until I said: How unreliable these people
> who refuse to grasp my ways!
> and so, in anger, I swore that not one
> would reach the place of rest I had for them.

In another translation the psalmist says:

For forty years I was wearied of these people
And I said: "Their hearts are astray,
These people do not know my ways."
Then I took an oath in my anger:
"Never shall they enter my rest".

In other words, as I get older and look back at the reality of my life I see more and more clearly how my life had wearied the Lord and yet, instead of casting me off completely, He spoke to me in a way that actually begat and began a new life. Thus, while I had one child lost to abortion, which I write about in this book, and which is a theme which occurs in the work of James Sale, my wife and I have ten children, two of whom went straight to heaven, owing to early miscarriages, and all of whom fell after each other in a hectic and exhausting first ten years and more of marriage.

But, as I often pray, if the Lord has been this merciful to me, speaking through my inability to hear and to respond to His word, then He can be equally or more merciful to others!

So, as I say, what began as a kind of commentary on James Sale's trilogy, *HellWard*, *StairWell*, and *DoorWay*, has evolved into a short book of reflections and recollections on the theme of the ongoing conversion which is integral to becoming Christian.

Chapter One

"Read! Repent! And Rejoice!": A Reflection on James Sale's Modernization of Dante's *Inferno*

Even the contemplation of Hell is a message of mercy in that it is the will of God that no one go there!

As James Sale says in an interview at the end of his book: '*it's not so much that God puts us there, but that we end up where we want to be*' (*HellWard*, p. 143[1]). Therefore, it is a mercy to see and stop where we have seen we could be going and to beg, if we are willing, to beg as beggars for the help of God to get us to heaven!

So, this short book is formed around three pieces, each of which responds to James Sale's modernization of Dante's trilogy; and, therefore, this first follows *Inferno* and is called *HellWard*.

---

[1] James Sale, *The English Cantos: Volume I: HellWard*, published by Amazon KDP, 2019.

Introduction: Pope Francis and James Sale

In part three of Pope Francis' letter on Dante, *Cantor Lucis Aeternae,* Francis says: 'by poetry, the art of the word which, by speaking to all, has the power to change the life of each' (3). Thus, we discover that the goal is so to depict the reality of sin and redemption so that all appeal to the mercy of God so generously expressed in Christ's forgiveness of sins (cf. Luke 23: 34) and receive the Spirit of the Resurrection (cf. John 20: 19-23). Thus, adapting the English translation of Dante to bring out its personal welcome of the sinner, this Lent and Easter, indeed every Lent and Easter and indeed in every "in-between", let us turn and turn again to what Dante describes as God's 'ample arms/ That ... receive whoever turns to him (*Purg.* III, 118-123)'.

If you, then, like me, need various helps into these great works read around, as I have done, and begin to see the almost palpable sense of discovering, through James Sale's near death experience, the reality of our life: here and hereafter. So, whether you read his autobiographical introduction or the interview at the end of his book, read what helps you enter this prose that strips what shows to show the glow of grace (cf. Sale, *HellWard*, p. 58) or its heinous absence!

Christ, Sale himself, and Dante

Although it is the 700th Anniversary of Dante's death, and various reference's to Dante's work abound, I confess to scarcely knowing very much about this poet and the first part of "The Divine Comedy": Dante's Inferno or Hell; indeed, I recall, that a comedy is not what we think it is, somewhat carelessly, a piece of light humour – rather a *Comedy* is an account of life which includes tragedy as well as triumph, where triumph, in this case, is not triumphalism but the victory of Love within us. Thus, *The Divine Comedy* is not only the scope or scape of human life opening upon eternity, of where Love triumphs but, in ghastly detail, it includes what it looks like when we reject the inner-work of God which would turn us to confession and to salvation.

As you might detect, then, from my opening words, the beginning of Sale's epic modernization of Dante's ancient account of life and death and all that ranges hence, from hell to purgatory to heaven, is a shocking depiction of what raw vice looks like – indeed to those, like me, unprepared for what is to come, the shock is somewhat akin to coming to the edge of a camp on a beautifully lit summer's day, bearing marks of what is still unclearly seen but suggesting, in ways that railway tracks and high barbed wire fencing might make you start to think about what is happening and still to come. And then the shock – not unlike the shock of seeing pictures of the aftermath of an atomic bomb; but not, as you might imagine, of how it impacts people we do not know but, rather, how it implicates those close to us and our relationship to them: my mother; my pupil; my boss; and so on to others in my life.

Imagine, then, like Christ says in the Gospel, between Lazarus and the rich man who did not help him there is a fixed divide which, even if we wanted to, we could not cross (cf. Lk 16: 19-31) and then, as I say, imagine that there is one whom we loved on the far side of this impossible divide and the anguish we go through as we cannot help – but can only pass on – and you will begin to experience what is depicted.

To take, then, but one of many examples, but one more compelling in that the poet tries to save his mother who, while he tries to lift her off her bed, and console her, discovers in the attempt the impossibility of freeing her from what, hiddenly, holds her fast:

To see her passive and in love with fate,
And those sheet folds around still clinging tight
Like coiling snakes who'd not discharge their
  freight

So much she loved them, and their toxic bite,
That God Himself – but then the plaster fell,
Showered our heads with dust and shattered bits

Could not undo the hell of her free will (Sale, *Hell-*
  Ward, pp. 14-15).

On the other hand, however, each of these people, some more widely known and named, either by name and deed or neither, may also be real in order to be rebuked lest they be lost; but then, again, they may be sufficiently imagined to stand for all who have power over the lives of others and waste, indescribably, the opportunity to love.

Dante as companion

So, Sale, the man who began to enter the bluey beauty of a *HeavenWard* thermal from the operating table and who yet returns, from glimpsing God, finds that he has not died and is no longer alone but is sent a companion, Dante himself, to accompany our modern poet on a downward journey – going *HellWard* all the more dramatically because of the prior brightness to which he rose, albeit so briefly, and on the basis of which the poet begins to see more clearly the possible realities of people he has loved but who are now unveiled from what, it seems, had hidden what they were really like. Thus, hell, as the place of unmasked human hearts bares, now bluntly, the corrupt attitudes and actions that a person has really brought to exist is all too clearly described and defined 'in season and out of season' (2 Tim 4: 2).

Thus, Sale gives us many striking instances of a strongly pulsed way of pitting words against our hardness of heart (cf. Ps 94) and, hopefully, piercing any complacency we may possess that Lent may enter in and unfold through Easter through the Resurrection of our Redeemer! So, on entering the room of what the poet had once thought to be a friend, and we are prepared for something disturbing in the preceding verses, we find that the wall is alive with embedded faces, expressing what we will discover as the verses continue beyond this excerpt, that his friend had fathered children without being a father to them:

> *'I'd knew you'd find me; knew you'd like my work.'*
> *What work? I thought. Then heard some sullen sobs:*
> *The walls themselves had faces in, each hurt –*
>
> *Each face half-formed, deformed, and like a yob's*
> *Made so through lack of love and fatherhood,*
> *But each one spoke, as one collective, mob;* (Sale, HellWard, p. 19).

So, what if this Lent we really ponder the possibility that we are that person we once thought we knew but are now nakedly evident for what we really are but, having hidden ourselves instead of availing ourselves of the sacrament of repentance and confession, we are now "stuck" with our unrepentant reality as we had rejected both our reality and its remedy of God's mercy – will it help us as this work is meant to do, to go to the physician for healing (cf. Lk 5: 31) before the complaint is set in an eternal, unreachable, fixity?

Just, however, as the descent seems to be unmitigated in its enfleshing of what is vicious within us we come upon the sudden change in Sale, as he descends, in such a wise as to intimate and then to announce a further, future brightening:

> *Thus Dante turned, to see me, who had died*
> *Almost, but now the corridor was lit*
> *Ahead from light my own being supplied.*
> *'Know,' Dante said, 'the grace is all of it;*
> *To waver one moment is to quench this flame*
> *Which out of you now flickers but a bit* (Sale,
> *HellWard*, p. 58).

And later, when Sale slumps, there is a good strong image of Dante jump starting Sale again.

Again, it is the contrast between both the various attempts to ruin Sale's life, and the overwhelming presence of an almost sweet word which spelt death for so many, that gives the one genuine friendship of his companion, Dante, reason to be there, it seems, to kick start Sale into life again:

> *To horrors here as was this fading gulf.*
> *And thinking so, as my whole weight went slump*
> *Against my teacher, I found his soul's stern proof*
>
> *Could hold me up, and its energy jump-*
> *Started my body with a vital power –*
> *As null and dull myself, and he the lamp* (Sale,
>   HellWard, p. 95).

In Conclusion

Altogether, then, we have many turns of phrase and stunning images which both help us now, in *HellWard*, to grasp the reality of our lives and, at the same time, press us forward with intimations of what is to come as Sale goes on to Purgatory and, eventually, to

Heaven in the two volumes of this modernization of Dante's *Divine Comedy* which are to follow.

From Pope Francis' Apostolic Letter on Dante, *Cantor Lucis Aeternae*, we have Dante's words with which to take us to our conclusion, both for James Sale and for us, words which tell us what rekindling the work of a great poet is about (5):

> "After I had my body lacerated
> By these two mortal stabs, I gave myself
> Weeping to Him, who willingly doth pardon.
> Horrible my iniquities had been;
> But Infinite Goodness hath such ample arms
> That it receives whatever turns to it"
>
> (*Purg.* III, 118-123)

Thus, we can see that even the contemplation of Hell is a message of mercy in that it is the will of God that no one go there! Thus, all poets who express this can say, adapting the words of Dante: 'by poetry, the art of the word which, by speaking to all, has the power to change the life of each' (*Cantor Lucis Aeternae*, 3) – to the good if graced by God! While still further we can widen the word of witness to announce, in any way by which the grace of God becomes visible, a word of salvation that, in saving us, hopes in the divine hope of saving others!

For those who want to know more about James Sale, his work and "The Wider Circle", go to: "The English Cantos: Journeys with Dante": https://englishcantos.home.blog/the-wider-circle/.

The prose and poem-prayer that follows, "Hell's Hole: An Unbidden Mercy" comes from *Within Reach of You: A Book of Prose and Prayers*: https://enroutebooksandmedia.com/withinreachofyou. This book was written very much out of the experience of Covid 19 and how our family life was structured by the practice of family prayer, the word of God, being a family of ten, and being able to go on walks together, pray together, and playing together. At the same time there are a variety of contributions from poets.

"Hell's-Hole: An Unbidden Mercy"

I do not remember when, exactly, this happened or the circumstances of my life at the time; but of this, I am sure, that it is a part of the Lord's mercy to warn us, from time to time, of the eternal significance of our actions. This prayer, then, arises out of one of the moments when, in a particularly vivid way, there arose an almost physical smell of despair – as if there was a place from which nothing escapes except the warning of its existence.

Whether, then, hell is an existential place, a place that exists or whether, in this instance, this was a grim glimpse of the full implications of my unforgiving heart and where, left unchanged, it would be forever chained to what it was – in one sense is irrelevant in that if hell is expressed as an irrevocable outcome of being unwilling to love, indeed to love my enemy (cf. Lk 6: 27-38), then it follows that hell will exist in being eternally expressed in me and, therefore, in being the "place" of all who will not escape the unforgivingness that can rise up or even "dwell in us".

However, being the kind of person I am, I was slow to appreciate the "gift" of this intimation of the reality of hopelessness. Indeed, it is almost as if, like the ancient Egyptians thought, the soul that was too heavy to rise sank – not because it was held down, put down or otherwise detained, as it were, but because the very nature of hopelessness is a kind of burying burdensomeness which, of itself, buries the very good of life itself and the many gifts of God given that it may bear abundant fruit (cf. Jn 10: 10).

There comes a point, then, in a person's life when, in the words of Scripture, God says: "What more could I have done for you?" (Is 5: 4). In other words, in front of God there will come a moment when I will see all that He has done to give me life and to bring me to salvation and, what is more, I will see all the help that I have resisted and, if I have, all the good I have done in cooperation with Him (cf. Jn 15: 5). In a word, then, I will not be able to hide behind resentment, injustice, complaints of any kind – but I will be bare of all excuses before the piercing glance of Love who has loved me!

"Hell's-Hole: An Unbidden Mercy"

Lord, for a moment, I stood alone amidst the
    odour of despair,
A glimpse I did not choose nor would entertain
    the thought of,

But, as if paring, parting, even disclosing the
    heart's going down,
Down, not to arise, burdened, soaked and inescapably sodden,
Sinking, stinking, slowly down, is where you
    showed me I was
Going, if not already gone, going down to be
    with the unwilling

To be unburdened (cf. Mt 11: 28-30), unforgivingness unburnt off,
Like a burden burning to be shed but unsheddable, unwillingness
Making it claustrophobically clinging, odourously rising,
Unrelentingly present, unrelievedly expressing
    what I chose in
Choosing un-loving: the inversion of the very
    heart of man.

Lord, for a moment, a hell-hole opened in my
    presence as if time
Was timed eternally, not in passing, briefly, as
    with this passing

Opening, but opening upon the horizon of what
   made hope
Hopeless: the impossible to describe endlessness
   of an undoable
Choice unable to be undone and doing, end-
   lessly, what it did:
Ending the possibility of a cleansing change: a
   relief that belongs to
Restoring health after an interminable illness
   only there is only
The interminable illness: the denaturing imper-
   fectability of being
Imprisoned in imperfections impossible to pass
   from, like an
Unshakeable smell, an interior collapsing of col-
   lapsed hoping: an
Incalculable uncountably interminably ever only
   present nowness.

Lord, for a moment, I saw the possibility of a
   transparent perception
Of my own heart's hearkening to itself and hug-
   ging a dreadful

Indwellingness which, unpeeled, bit upon
   blooms beyond telling a
Happiness unreachable, unlovingness un-
   quenchable, mercy refused
A refuse remaining, a shrivelling intimation of
   the swelling of what
Could have been grown to the full and full to
   burgeoning, breaking
Upon a gratitude eternally opening, ever freshly
   bursting, rising and
Never dying, rejoicing untiringly, telling and
   telling out again and
Again the glory to be given to God if only – if
   only loving had been
Opened, little by little, loving by loving, day by
   day eternally being
The beginning promised and still promised if
   today I listen (cf. Ps 95).

Chapter Two

Jesus said to Him: "Get Up, Pick Up Your Mat and Walk" (John 5: 8): A Reflection on James Sale's *StairWell*

Introduction: When Change is a Gift of God

Helen Roseveare said: "God never uses a person greatly until He has wounded him deeply"[1]. On the one hand, there is James Sale's 'real battle with cancer', an encounter with his 'ex-wife' and the loss of a child to 'abortion' (*StairWell*, Foreword, Evan Mantyk, p. xii, xiii and Sale, p. 40 ff). On the other hand, what God allows because He can bring good out of it is not the same as what God causes to exist: 'St. Thomas explains that ... "God allows evils to be done in order to draw forth some greater good"'[2]. At the same time,

---

[1] Helen Roseveare: https://www.azquotes.com/quote/533895

[2] St. Thomas Aquinas, *Summa theologiae*, 3, 1, 3 and 3; cf. CCC, 412, quoted in *The Navarre Bible: Pentateuch*, p. 55.

while a number of these authors would be unknown to Dante Alighieri (1265-1321), St. Thomas Aquinas (1224-1274) would be well known to him as he was Dante's teacher – both well versed in faith and reason and, therefore, inspiring the like in his pupil[3]. We have, then, Sales own faith journey which, currently, has taken him to the Anglican Church[4]; and, therefore, there is a sense that we are reading, in *StairWell,* an account of encountering the mercy of Christ which is clearly at the root of Dante's own inspiration[5].

Pope Francis quotes Dante's beautiful expression, saying:

"But infinite Goodness hath such ample arms
That it receives whatever turns to it" (*Purg*. III,
    118-123)' (5).

---

[3] Benedict XV, *In Praeclara Summorum,* 4, https://www.vatican.va/content/benedict-xv/en/encyclicals/documents/hf_ben-xv_enc_30041921_in-praeclara-summorum.html.

[4] Email correspondence with James Sale, 11/01/2023.

[5] Pope Francis' letter on Dante, *Cantor Lucis Aeternae,* https://press.vatican.va/content/salastampa/it/bollettino/pubblico/2021/03/25/0181/00393.html#ing.

While the problem of translation abounds, Dante is clearly referring to the Lord "who" receives whoever 'turns' to Him! But does not just turn to Him but, like the father in the parable of the prodigal son (cf. Lk 15: 20) – embraces all who turn to Him in His 'ample arms'!

Thus, whether like Pope Francis and his predecessors, Dante, Sale or myself, who have been saved in the embrace of those 'ample arms' of the Lord, or whether you are still striving for the freeing truth (cf. Jn 8: 32) or even, in the spirit of this work, you are yet to encounter even the possibility of this meeting – this work is for all and at every stage of starting and even those of us, especially, who are well behind the starting line! How fitting, then, that Dante accompanies Sale, the poet, throughout his journey upward. What, then, an auspicious and momentous task: to modernize an awakening to the truth, the call to conversion: to an encounter with God!

Where to go from here? To go back in order to go forward!

To continue, then, this is Sale's second volume of Dante's trilogy, *Inferno*, *Purgatorio* and *Paradiso*, otherwise known as the *Divine Comedy*; and, so, Sale started with *HellWard* and he is now ascending through *StairWell* and is going on to *DoorWay*[6].

It is argued that the *Divine Comedy*, 'inaugurated realism and self-portraiture in modern fiction'[7]. Indeed, if there is a kind of realism, it is a superrealism to which Sale appeals, dramatically and effectively, as his account demonstrates.

Speaking of his mother's death, Sale lets her recount the moment of her death as a part of her narrative response, as it were, to what her life has been about:

> 'I coughed so gently, just two times, before
> The nurse worked out my heart, indeed, had
>   stopped;

---

[6] Email correspondence with James Sale, 29/06/2023.

[7] By Eric Auerbach, cited in the *Divine Comedy*: https://en.wikipedia.org/wiki/Divine_Comedy.

> And while they fussed – the doctor through the door –
> My spirit spun in spirals ever down
> Through blackness in a blackened corridor'
> (*StairWell*, p. 23).

Sale's realism, an embracing realism, which includes his mother's account of her own death and as a part of which she gives the impression that all is lost: 'My spirit spun in spirals ever down/Through blackness in a blackened corridor'.

Sale then goes on to say that his mother met her mother who had tormented her; but, instead of blaming Sale's grandmother, his mother says, 'But mine is not to blame' (*StairWell*, p. 24). Thus, the death of his mother has a kind of "break" about it: the almost chain reaction of generational harm being "broken" by his mother's pause, saying, 'But mine is not to blame'. Thus, death is an expansive moment, to be expanded both before and after, as it were, not as a "passing death" but indicating a saving, spiritual event. And this is the point. The realism which is spoken of here is not to be confused with a banal and empty empiricism which, for all its name, stands for the contradiction of "materialism": an account of reality that cannot account for own existence as an explanation of what exists. Rather, Sale's realism is an encompassing one, communicating the rich and complex reality of human experience: the full import of which is told throughout his poetry and drawing on its ancient roots.

The theme of his mother, from hell to purgatory

Starting with an excerpt from my review of *Hell-Ward*, Sale's first Canto, and an excerpt from it that goes with it, I then take up the theme of Sale's relationship to his mother as it strikes out afresh in *Stair-Well*[8].

'To take, then, but one of many examples, but one more compelling in that the poet tries to save his mother who, while he tries to lift her off her bed, and console her, discovers in the attempt the

---

[8] Cf. Etheredge, review of James Sale's *HellWard*, https://www.hprweb.com/2021/12/book-reviews-january-2022/#cantos.

impossibility of freeing her from what, hiddenly, holds her fast:

To see her passive and in love with fate,
And those sheet folds around still clinging tight
Like coiling snakes who'd not discharged their freight

So much she loved them, and their toxic bite,
That God Himself – but then the plaster fell,
Showered our heads with dust and shattered bits –
Could not undo the hell of her free will (Sale, *Hell-Ward*, pp. 14-15).'

But when Sale recounts his encounter with his mother, in *StairWell*, there is a superbly vivid image of a person searching, but not abstractly, for what really matters – but in the very flesh of her existence. At the same time, this gives the reason, as it were, his mother did not remain in hell, where hell is understood in a wide, biblical sense, of being the place before Christ's appearance after the *Resurrection* releases those trapped there. Nevertheless, there is still the meaning of hell as a place "inescapable" to which

I shall refer in due course. Here, though, given the context of Dante saying to Sale that "'You are about,' ..., 'to find love'" (*StairWell*, p. 20), wherein both mother and son ask each other for forgiveness (*StairWell*, p. 21), Sale says of encountering his mother, that

> 'A holy wailing wrapped me in in its cask;
> So solid, pain was tangible – visible –
> Peeling the skin as acid might a mask:
>
> Wherein – I saw her – clawing for her soul,
> Stripping away the layers plastered there
> Through years, which now in shreds, plopped in
>   the bowl
>
> Beneath her bed,' (*StairWell*, p. 20).

Thus, an account both vivid and, paradoxically, understated: that of his mother searching her own flesh 'for her soul' which, as she does so, plops 'in the bowl/Beneath her bed'. A truly evocative image, especially considering the "Word made flesh" (Jn 1: 14) which entered into the real human history of lived experience and, illuminating it from within, makes it possible for us to see the significance buried, as it were, in the flesh of experience. It is possible, therefore, that the flesh that is here described as 'plopped in the bowl' is that bloated corruption of our appetites that both destroy us and those with whom we come into contact; as, in the end, other people are either "used up" in a kind of consumption of pleasure or they are the "but" of our gross self-ignorance. But what redeems these awful pages is the call to communion, within the very family that seemed to have disfigured Sale so; and, indeed, even as he passes on, he is called to pray for them and bring them, as it were, with him albeit according to the pace of their own salvation (cf. *StairWell*, p. 29).

We have, then, this beautiful plea for prayer, by Sale's mother, that what is broken in family life can be healed in the life of the Christian family:

> 'She paused. 'Pray James, for me, and pray in full -
> Pray every time your eyes close, while you live;
> Pray, knowing nothing deflects His searching will

> That will not be gainsaid its harvest – love.
> Inscrutable His majesty and power;
> My heart yearns to suffer and be above
>
> With Him where, at last, He will tread the hours
> To dust, and we will freely be like Him.'
>
> Her speech astonished me – certain, assured'
> (*StairWell*, p. 27).

Thus, the pages describe this encounter, which includes the loving forgiveness she denied her husband on his deathbed but now attends to him, as she can (*StairWell*, pp. 24-25). In so doing, Sale includes the whole psychological drama of words uttered in a vile way that bear a destructive virus and, what is more, the spiritual battle entailed in not being destroyed by them shows the presence of the transforming grace of God as how we suffer accounts, exactly, for what is needed to restore the wholesomeness of human love which, in reality, is divinized when it is completely fulfilled. And if it is supposed that these accounts are, as it were, fanciful, I can testify that through years of different kinds of sufferings, whether it be psychological crises, spiritual promptings to go to confession and listen to His word, the compelling impulse to pray, four operations, never mind the almost destruction of my legs from blood clots, through the blocked blood attacking them (varicose eczema) – these sufferings are experienced by the whole person who, as they are experienced, seeks the connection to his life and sinfulness and the mercy of God: the years of resisting forgiveness and nursing "unforgiveness" and forgetting and forging sins, the reality of which has a brutally biting impact on others[9].

As the journey continues so we discover the hitherto secret reason that Sale's mother is not a permanent resident in hell, 'Where those persist who cannot change their fate' (*StairWell*, p. 31), as Dante explains:

'How late your prayers' potent efficacies

---

[9] Cf. various books by Etheredge, notably and simply, *The Prayerful Kiss*: https://enroutebooksandmedia.com/theprayerfulkiss/; *Honest Rust and Gold: A Second Collection of Prose and Poetry*: https://enroutebooks andmedia.com/honestrustandgold/.

(Were laid and willed before the world was
   made)
Transport your mother finally to bliss.'

I stood stunned: this gift, an unworldly trade,
That One above whose mercy knows no measure,
Released her because – and I wept – I prayed
   (*StairWell*, p. 32).

Hell and suffering: Purgatory and Suffering

C. S. Lewis says vividly: '"To enter heaven is to become more human than you ever succeeded in being on earth; to enter hell is to be banished from humanity. What is cast (or casts itself) into hell is not a man: it is 'remains'"[10]

In Dante's work, 'Each sin's punishment in *Inferno* is a contrapasso, a symbolic instance of poetic justice; for example, in Canto XX, fortune-tellers and soothsayers must walk with their heads on

---

[10] C. S. Lewis quotes: https://libquotes.com/c-s-lewis/quote/lbk9s6n.

backwards, unable to see what is ahead, because that was what they had tried to do in life:

> '... and since he wanted so to see ahead,
> he looks behind and walks a backward path'[11].

However true that maybe of a sinner suffering in Dante's *Inferno*, and I seem to recall that there was a definite influence on Sale in his first Canto, *Hell-Ward*, what that account demonstrates, as it were, is the "logic" of hell as a permanent state of repudiation: of that terrible despair of ever loving or being loved that those who have irrevocably rejected forgiving or being forgiven experience in that they are "trapped in their sin". Nevertheless, even if there is a "poetic justice" in that the suffering of sin can be expressed in such a way that its "spiritual secret" is shown through a specific torment, two things need to be addressed.

---

[11] *Inferno*, Canto XX, lines 13–15 and 38–39, Mandelbaum translation, quoted in the Wikipedia article, *Divine Comedy* (cited previously).

Firstly, suffering is also remedial and, through the action of God, it is about calling us to conversion – even the terrible sufferings depicted in the *Book of Revelation* are an expression, paradoxically, of the divine desire that no one be lost.

> 'However, as with our own, personal sufferings, so with the sufferings we go through as a community, as a world-community, the good the Lord seeks to bring out of it all is the good of our eternal salvation (cf. Ps 7: 12; Ez 11: 1-21 and 38: 21-23; and Rev 9: 20-21 and Jn 3: 16-21)'[12].

Secondly, there is the great question of the suffering of the innocent. Indeed, in view of the growing warmth between the Catholic Church and the Jewish People, mediated by the three Initiators of the *Neocatechumenal Way*, one of them, Kiko Argüello [13], composed a symphony on the theme of the *Suffering*

---

[12] Short extract from Francis Etheredge, *An Unlikely Gardener*, En Route Books and Media, 2023.

[13] The other two are Fr. Mario Pezzi and Carmen Hernandez.

of the Innocents, especially remembering those who lost their lives in the Concentration Camps of the Second World War[14]. It also seems, however, that this theme runs deeply in Kiko's life and was a part of his conversion to the Catholicism he inherited:

> 'In the early 1960s, Francisco José Gómez Argüello (Kiko), a Spanish painter, winner of the Special National Painting Prize in 1959, after a deep existential crisis, discovered in the suffering of the innocents the mystery of Christ Crucified, who is present in the last ones of the earth This experience led him to abandon everything and, following in the footsteps of Charles de Foucauld, he went to live among the poor in Palomeras Altas'[15].

Thus, we come to Jesus Christ, the suffering *Innocent One*, and how our redemption follows on His divine, risen presence among us, both historically

---

[14] Cf. for example, https://www.youtube.com/watch?v=9FAfVz4ZUaI.

[15] "What is the Neocatechumenal Way": https://neocatechumenaleiter.org/en/history/.

and sacramentally, in the mysteries of the Catholic Church. And, while we could dwell further on other aspects of this work, perhaps it is timely to draw this piece to a close and to point, as it were, in the direction of heaven through that coming *DoorWay* Sale is now working on.

In conclusion, then, while there are both allusions to classical figures which escape me and, at the same time, questions of poetic competence which are completely beyond me[16], it is clear from reading and re-reading *StairWell* that Sale, like Dante, succeeds in the basic task which is a participation in the divine work 'to raise mortals from the state of misery ... and lead them to the state of happiness':

> 'Dante's work, Pope Francis says, shows eloquently and effectively "how false it is to say that obedience of mind and heart to God is a hindrance to genius, which instead it spurs

---

[16] There are plenty of references and notes at the end of *StairWell* for those who want to pursue the classical allusions and to investigate the structure of the poetry, pp. 175-196.

on and elevates". For this reason, the Pope continued, "the teachings bequeathed to us by Dante in all his works, but especially in his threefold poem", can serve "as a most precious guide for the men and women of our own time", particularly students and scholars, since "in composing his poem, Dante had no other purpose than to raise mortals from the state of misery, that is from the state of sin, and lead them to the state of happiness, that is of divine grace'" (Part I)[17].

Finally, the poignant reflection on Sale's relationship to his mother and, in the course of the whole book, others whom he has known, brings out the contrast between death being a non-event and a divine opportunity, taking us beyond the 'millions moaning in their dull/Lament, which I for sure wanted to leave' (*StairWell*, pp. 33-34). If we, then, you and I, come to Sale's text with our lives and ponder all that this journey entails, maybe we can have the possibility, too, of being reconciled where we

---

[17] Pope Francis' letter on Dante, *Cantor Lucis Aeternae,* Part I.

thought reconciliation was impossible knowing, in the end, that nothing is impossible to God (Lk 1: 37). Moreover, without disrespect to Sale but, rather, in keeping with the impulse of the commemoration of Dante's work you might, like me, seek a copy, even in translation, of Dante's *Divine Comedy* and hope to discover afresh whatever is to be found there, having trod upon a *StairWell* that goes that way!

In what follows, there are thoughts about stairs and how we do not necessarily get on a staircase at the same point; but, nevertheless, there is always an opportunity to do – unless we slam the door in the face of Christ and His disciples. But even then, maybe there is still the possibility of repentance. For, if there can be such an outpouring of prayer when a person commits suicide, maybe in the dying there was a regret through which the mercy of God could show itself. And, therefore, it is not for us to say who is lost or who is too late to take a step in the right direction. And thinking of stairs, I was thinking too of Mary, the Mother of the Lord, encouraging anyone and everyone to start the ascent towards her son, Jesus Christ.

"Oh Mother of the Stairs"

Albeit briefly, many years ago I was put in a prison cell while the police decided what to do with me; as, wandering the countryside, I was obviously thought to be on drugs or mentally ill. What had happened was that failing to get on with my university course, failing to form friendships, not knowing what to do next and absolutely tormented by questions about the purpose and meaning of life, I put the keys to my lodgings back through the front door as I left to go. I did not know where. I ended up in a cell and, after a while, on a psychiatric ward for a few weeks. However, even this brief experience makes me think of the solid cells, their sheer walls, formidable doors and intermittent visits by staff. So, although this does not equate with the full extent of a prison sentence, it is a real and personal point of departure.

"I don't know how much you know about the Covid situation in prison but it's pretty grim – no visits, locked inside cells for 23 hours a day, huge increase in self harm especially in women's prisons, pretty much all education, rehabilitation, recreation, gym sessions have been put on hold. They've managed to contain it so far but there's a lot of concerns that prisons are too full for proper distancing or safety measures – they're near capacity anyway, and there isn't enough staff. Some campaigners are trying to push for early releases for those with short sentences or who are waiting for their trials in order to reduce the pressure, but not much is being done even though it's been agreed as necessary and a few were released back in the summer when the less infectious variant was the main worry"[18].

---

[18] Courtesy of Teresa Etheredge, email, 14/1/2021, studying Criminology at University, England; see, also, "Prisoners to entrepreneurs: Business holds the key to reducing re-offending."

The Centre for Entrepreneurs explains the rationale behind turning prisoners into business owners...": *by Maximilian Yoshioka,* Updated: Jun 9, 2016 Published: Jun 9, 2016: https://startups.co.uk/blog/turning-prisoners-into-entrepreneurs-why-business-holds-the-key-to-reducing-reoffending/.

Chapter Two : «Get Up, Pick Up Your Mat and Walk» 51

In addition, then, to the considerations raised by my daughter, there is a real need to approach the situation of prisoners with practical compassion; indeed, it might even begin with simple advice, based on my own experience. Thus, to offset long periods of inactivity with short periods, around fifteen minutes, of legs been put up against a wall to help to change the blood circulating through them – even going as far as cycling in the air. Furthermore, drawing on my son's experience, even doing the same with hands.

At the same time as developing the possibility of promoting a care system that prevents deterioration, there could be cultural helps that contribute to this, beginning with a type of music that would go with a more meditative style of exercise. What about growing plants from seeds? I know from watching the potatoes that have started to shoot, when they are put on the windowsill in the kitchen, they start to turn dark green and show the beginnings of being plants; indeed, how amazing it is that chlorophyll develops in the pale shoots simply because of sunlight? What questions could arise in the mind of a person locked in a cell contemplating the growth of a plant? Would it bring out the scientist, the poet or the gardener in them (or all three)? Certainly, there are security challenges and the whole problem of who can be trusted with what – but what about the challenge of a little work to grow food, flowers or even cultivate a business mentality? Furthermore, then, there are the questions of hope, of one person being linked up to help another, of the specific help that a person needs who is contemplating suicide or harming another person. In other words, there is all the more reason for the necessity of going beyond the difficulties and rising to the challenges of the situation.

This, clearly, is an important work for ex-offenders, chaplains and volunteers who are able to engage, positively, with the imperative of taking people forward in their lives and not just because of the short-term necessity of help, as valid as that is. Thus, while it is self-evident that there are concerns for the well-being of prisoners, staff and the public generally, there are also humanitarian goals that go beyond the limitations of the situation and call for new ways forward. Who knows what untapped resources remain dormant or require the motivation to transfer skills from crime to the good to be done - in the prisoners themselves?!

What about a parish adoption of a prison or a prison block? Where, at the very least, the prisoners are prayed for regularly; and, who knows, what as yet unknown good works will spring from such seeds?

"Oh Mother of The Stairs"

You inherited a title from our first mother, Eve,
    and, as the New Eve, you are even more the mother of all the living, loving
To call out to all to take the steps to life, to enter from whatever
Turning point and to take the rail, the rhythm of life and prayer
And to ascend, step by step, holding on as you are helped to hold
On and to rise, and rise again, rising in the company of others.

Oh Joseph, as you worked you saw who was lost and looking around,

And you prayed, whether in words or gestures,
   dedicating your
Difficulties to turning boys and girls, youths, old
   men and women,
To your wife, Mary, who stands by the entrance
   to the stairs,
Calling to all who would pass on by to stop, to
   falter just in time,
And to follow the turning up, and to avoid the
   turning down.

Oh Mother of the Stairs, let not those who are
   on the money-go-round
Stay stuck on the cutting edge, getting caught up
   in the swirling
Down and round, round and down until, either
   fished up or flat
Against the possibility of the water-fall, taking
   them beyond the
Edge of returning, descending without drown-
   ing, falling as they
Fail, failing as they fall, faster now, unless netted
   before the end.

Oh Lord, you have descended to hell and you have ascended
To heaven, you know the way down and you know the way up;
And, indeed, you know all the steps in between and all the
Stops and starts and changes of direction, encouraging all
Who are going down to come up and all who are going up to
Continue up, and even as they go to help others to rise with them.

You knew imprisonment and you turned it into an opportunity
For the salvation of the world; you knew the isolation of being
Intensely alone and again you turned it into an opportunity
For the salvation of the world; you knew the utter worn-out-ness
Of carrying your cross and bearing afflictions for others and you

Turned it into an opportunity for the salvation
  of the world.

Help all who are imprisoned bear the burden of
  illness, isolation,
Even estrangement, turning their cross into op-
  portunities to shed
Addictions, to see in their lives your Son's walk
  with them to the
Resurrection, to turn around and see the good-
  ness of God coming
Towards them, arms outstretched, bringing the
  healing love that
Loves to heal, turning them up-wards to go up
  the stairs with help.

Oh Mother of the Stairs, gather your children
  from all walks of life,
All points of the earth, all peoples of the world,
  all times of life,
Whether poor or rich, victim or violent, alone or
  as part of a gang,
Turning what is misused to a good use, schem-
  ing into helping,

Gang members into friends, taking into giving,
  causing harm
Into helping to heal – being saved into showing
  others the stairs[19].

---

[19] Published in the "Prison Challenges" edition of "Profiles in Catholicism": https://www.catholicprofiles.org/post/april-15-2021-profile-in-catholicism; and "Oh Mother of the Stairs" is from an excerpt from pp. 174-180 of *Within Reach of You: A Book of Prose and Prayers*: https://enroutebooksandmedia.com/withinreachofyou/.

Chapter Three

"DoorWay" to 'The Lord of All'[1]:
A Reflection on James Sale's *DoorWay*

I have been rather slow to decide how to respond to this book, the third in James Sale's contemporary re-write of Dante's trilogy on *Hell*, which he called *HellWard*, *Purgatory*, which he called *StairWell*, and *Heaven*, which he has called *DoorWay*. On the one hand, my impression of *DoorWay* has been settled for some time. Indeed, setting heaven amongst the stars, amidst the "star-signs" of the Zodiac, has struck me as an imaginative setting, allowing heaven to be both mystical and "above", with all that entails in terms of the mystery of God's presence and the spiritual transportation which is intimately a part of this "spiritual place" in which there are 'many mansions' (John 14: 2). On the other hand, however, my thinking about what to focus on has now crystallized on

---

[1] James Sale, *The English Cantos: Volume III: Door-Way*, independently published, printed by Amazon , 2025, pp. 172, including notes, pp. 141-172, Canto 9: "Arriving in Aquarius", p. 123.

the subject of the butterfly. The butterfly had already appeared in the second book, *StairWell* and, in the Foreword by Evan Mantyk, we learn that the butterfly has a very personal significance for James Sale: that of a child of his lost to abortion[2].

Introduction: Why the theme of the 'butterfly'?

But, before I proceed further, it might be asked why I am focusing on this subject when, overall, it is but one motif amongst many in this modern account of both the spiritual life and the characteristics of the society through which we move: Whether "Up" or "Down"? Because, in another sense, the death and salvation of all, of anyone, of each one of us, is not only a profoundly personal journey, rooted in the actual reality of our life – but it is the pilgrimage that none can escape and all must embrace. If, by contrast, we manage to deny that we will die, disown our

---

[2] *StairWell*, Foreword, Evan Mantyk, p. xii, xiii and Sale, p. 40 ff; and, indeed, my own experience can be found in a poem called "Indelible", in the book *The Prayerful Kiss*: https://www.amazon.co.uk/Prayerful-Kiss-Collection-Poetry-Prose-ebook/dp/B07V8L33VT.

own actions, good or bad, or live as if this life is all there is, then we need this Sale's trilogy to takes us through an actual encounter with death, and which leads to the questions on which rests, literally, the infinitely long outcome of hell, or purgatory as a preparation for heaven. As Professor Joseph S. Salemi says in his *Introduction* to *DoorWay*: 'finite acts have infinite implications'[3]. In other words, the theme of *DoorWay* is both the third book of a trilogy, that of encountering heaven, but it can double as an appeal to all who need to hear the poet's words:

> 'Your words, through His Spirit, tell of His glories
> To peoples who have yet to see the sun
> And live. If art be true, your words won't miss'[4].

Thus, this way of utter self-scrutiny can be a *DoorWay* to Heaven! As the author says: 'His baptismal plunge strips away the remnants of sin and

---

[3] *DoorWay*, "Introduction", p. xiii.
[4] *DoorWay*, "Canto 2: Family Scales", p. 23.

decay, drawing him into the transformative power of grace'[5].

> 'So now the Cherub met me in the depths
> Of baptism new, for my life to begin,
>
> Stripping off me the body's deadening crepe,
> Impurities seventy years or more
> Crustacean-like, had formed in slime's still
>   sloth'[6].

In the first place, my reason for this focus is that the poet himself has drawn attention to what is in our midst; and, having addressed it both personally and in terms of what exists in our society, it is there to be recognized in both being rarely and poignantly pictured. The reality in our time is that abortion proceeds unabated and, if anything, has been multiplying the harm done as its insatiable appetite finds more and more ways to end the lives of children. For, through abortion pills, the bathroom at home has been turned into an abortuary; and, for many

---

[5] *DoorWay*, Canto 1: St. Dismas Speaks, p. 1.
[6] *DoorWay*, Canto 1: St. Dismas Speaks, p. 4.

women, it has become a place of "triggering", not to mention the multiple harms to multiple women which are constantly surfacing. My second reason for touching on this subject is the contrast between Sale's vivid depiction of the savagery of abortion and the tenderness that arises out of considering the image of his child as a 'butterfly'. The savagery of abortionists and their torment in *HellWard* is enough to frighten; and, in that the fear of God is the beginning of wisdom, this is not unhelpful. By contrast, the 'butterfly' evokes the slightest, flimsiest creature which certainly corresponds to the scarcely present but actual, existent reality, of the real person real from the first instant of conception. But more than that, as we shall see, the 'butterfly' is a delight, both to the poet, and in itself has the power and the potential of that power to be healing: to bring comfort and encouragement to those, like Sale, who have suffered this unforgettable loss.

My third and final reason for addressing this subject is a document of the *Catholic Church* on the future, literally, of children who die without *Baptism*. In other words, there is a wonderful coincidence between Sale's affirmation of the existence of his child in heaven and the direction of the *Catholic Church's* doctrinal understanding of the mercy of God.

Part I:
Retracing my steps:
HellWard and StairWell

But first I want to retrace my steps back to *Hell-Ward*, however briefly, in which Sale depicts in an awful scene, in page after page, the experience of a man called Kip who sold his sperm for money[7]. Moreover, a 'harpy' appears later in this scene and says to him, 'you raped me' and proceeds to torture Kip[8], the ugliness of this evocation of the sins of the flesh is thereby totally intensified. The harpy, taken from mythology, is a vicious female faced form which punishes a king 'for his ill-treatment of his children'[9]. In other words, the impression Sale creates is of the gravity of a sinner's selfish acts which so distort a man as to produce a graphic grotesqueri-

---

[7] *HellWard: Revisited*, Canto 3: Pupil, p. 24.

[8] *HellWard: Revisited*, Canto 3: Pupil, p. 28.

[9] "Harpy: mythology": https://www.britannica.com/topic/Harpy.

sation of him who became a father of fatherless beings, yet still justified all he did for money. The proportionate space in which these deeds are depicted, begins to suggest that so many more sins are implicated here. And thus the thoughts that come to mind are of all those acts, seemingly detached from humanity, whereby children are conceived in glass dishes, in surrogate mothers, in violent ways, as if all the while there is no consequence for the oft-hidden man who sells, donates or drives his semen upon women. The inward reality of the man, and that of all who directly contribute to this dehumanizing process, of making money from selecting and de-selecting children, is profoundly ruptured in his humanity – no matter what the outward semblance of respectability or business-like exterior the whole tragedy assumes.

And so, in *HellWard*, there is the following account of a sin and its consequences; indeed, the very title of the book suggests that this false fathering of children is an action tending to hell. And, so, Sale suggests that the children so conceived are somehow unformed through the 'lack of love and fatherhood' which rightly belonged to their being given existence.

At the same time, while they may not be actual children, trapped as they are in a terrible forever state, yet these children may be an indication of the deformity of the man's fatherhood and, as such, are a kind of iconic presence the frustration of his own fatherhood that he cannot escape.

'The walls themselves had faces in, each hurt –

Each face half-formed, deformed, and like a yob's
Made so through lack of love and fatherhood,
But each one spoke, as one collective, mob'[10].

So, what has this to do with the 'butterfly' that, in the third book, *DoorWay*, flutters about while yet leading his father purposely through heaven? By implication, then, the abortion of a child is implicated in the torments described in *HellWard*; for, if a tragic destruction of humanity falls upon those who contributed to father-less children, what will become of those who contributed to their death – either by vacuum cleaner, dismembering, or some pseudo medicalization of a non-illness? Therefore, by contrast,

---

[10] *HellWard: Revisited*, Canto 3: Pupil, p. 23.

Chapter Three : «DoorWay » to « The Lord of All»   67

there is a redeeming work of rescuing a father's love of his lost son.

And so this is what we encounter in *StairWell*, the pain of knowing what had happened and how we suffer, whether as the mother who aborts her child or the father who knows. Thus, the poet meets the woman, his ex-wife, who aborted their son.

> 'Hari', I blurted, 'ivory's real bone:
> That child we had together, you destroyed,
> His flesh and blood consumed, and his souls
>   gone[11].

And at the same time as the reality of what happened hurts, so it seems to bring forth a number of transformations: of a fly that emerges from the disfigured mother which yet transforms into a butterfly; a longing of frustrated fatherhood, turned to rejoicing; and a new beginning begotten in purgatory, for the mother, the father, and indeed the child. Each are in some way changed, not least the child which seemed to have shed his experience of being bur-

---

[11] *StairWell*, Canto 3: Ex-Wife, p. 41.

dened, aborted, as if some foul 'fly'[12], and is now 'so beautiful, so light', 'so fragile, free in flight'.

> 'The clinic killing and the wrong she knew
> She'd done dead child of whom I only dream,
> How in my heart my being longs for you!'[13]

> 'The fly no longer one now took to wing,
> A butterfly so beautiful, so light,
> So graceful, its sight induced in me song
>
> Charged and transported I'd made paradise,
> At least in that moment. I wondered hard
> To see it soar so fragile, free in flight'[14].

Thus, as we finally get to the third book, *Door-Way*, we have a history of transformations which are either complete or in the process of completion; and, in particular, the fly become butterfly, now flits in and out of the pages that follow.

---

[12] *StairWell*, Canto 3: Ex-Wife, pp. 42-44.
[13] *StairWell*, Canto 3: Ex-Wife, p. 42.
[14] *StairWell*, Canto 3: Ex-Wife, p. 44.

But, by way of a pause, before continuing this theme, there is a brief interlude wherein what has happened to the fly now 'A butterfly so beautiful, so light, So graceful, its sight induced in me a song'.

Part II:
A Theological Reflection and a Poet's Intuition

James Sale is an Anglican and may very well not be aware as I, as a Catholic, that there was an idea in the Catholic Tradition that was, in effect, an attempt to answer a dilemma that arose. Baptism is necessary to remedy the defect of original sin, which in itself makes us unacceptable to be in the presence of God, even if the child has not personally sinned. Thus, not deserving hell, nor able to enter heaven, as unbaptized, it was supposed that there was an eternal, natural happiness.

In view, however, of a new investigation, there is now a new mentality of the Church which embraces the child who, through no fault of his or her own, dies without baptism. Thus, the *Catechism of the Catholic Church* says: 'As regards children who have died without Baptism, the Church can only entrust them to the mercy of God, as she does in her funeral rites for them' (CCC, 1261). Naturally, then, this does not dispense from the obligation to baptize, if at all possible, whether in the ordinary or extra ordinary situations of life. But it does signify a rejection of the idea of limbo, which was defined as a natural state of the unbaptized and, as such, neither that of heaven nor hell, in that limbo has now been dropped from the teaching of the Church and is not even mentioned in the new *Catechism*[15].

James Sale, then, in his whole depiction of the relationship between himself and his son, the 'butterfly', has a father's and a poet's presentiment of the embracing mercy of God. In other words, there was no uncertainty for him: the butterfly is indeed in heaven and even seems to have a purpose in drawing his father on, to follow from *StairWell* into *DoorWay*: from purgatory into heaven:

'But that dear butterfly, like some lost boat,

---

[15] *The Hope of Salvation for Infants who Die without being Baptised*: https://www.vatican.va/roman_curia/congregations/cfaith/cti_documents/rc_con_cfaith_doc_20070419_un-baptised-infants_en.html#_ftnref130.

Had left the harbour of my hand to swivel
Elsewhere, and out of sight, while I had turned –
How find my love?'[16]

And that perhaps is the answer: that a father who loves imitates the Father who is Love and knows that a child innocent of personal sin cannot be lost to the presence of God.

Part III: The Poignancy of the Butterfly

And so, while the butterfly is not the main subject and yet, like a family in a kind of hide and seek which stimulates the seeker as in the *Song of Songs*, so his son has a purpose:

'This butterfly behind your back who hovers,
Awaits you patient on that higher plane'[17].

---

[16] *DoorWay*, Canto 1: St. Dismas Speaks, p. 8.
[17] *DoorWay*, Canto 3: Constellation of the Virgin, p. 41.

And, by way of explanation, the butterfly moves according to an inner compass which, guiding the child himself, guides his father too:

'Whom I did seek: a head of me, light-years,
My Butterfly, obliquely flying home,
In-built that Love which his course he steers'[18].

And now, if I am not mistaken, although there are many detours, at last the poet's son speaks,

'But 'Father!' and my soul revived – to hear
His voice, to see him now living again,
With such compassion from him to me, clear!'[19].

We then discover that the child has brought his father to the 'living God': 'To bless the past despite my looking back'[20]. Thus, there is an unhelpful and an unhealthy regret that does not reconcile us to our past – but which grace of reconciliation is the work of the 'living God that brought me here'.

---

[18] *DoorWay*, Canto 5: Waters of the Crab, p. 66.
[19] *DoorWay*, Canto 6: Fire of the Archer, p. 69-70.
[20] *DoorWay*, Canto 6: Fire of the Archer, p. 70.

But the poet's son does not just speak with compassion, reviving his father, but seems to grow in flesh: a flesh that had scarcely begun before his life was aborted[21]. And, therefore, there is a kind of son-to-father embrace that, contrary to what we would expect, seems to make the father seem 'unreal' to himself by comparison – but, at the same time, 'A pain, yes, but ones all designed to heal'[22]. In order, then, for the poet to fulfil that longing of holding his own son, he realizes

> 'But that to sacrifice my own existence
> Was necessary were I to hold my son'[23].

And yet the son can hold his father on an 'eagle's back':

> 'By arms belonging to my own dear son
> I found myself, and his blessing, gone'[24].

---

[21] *DoorWay*, Canto 6: Fire of the Archer, pp. 68-69.

[22] *DoorWay*, Canto 6: Fire of the Archer, p. 71.

[23] *DoorWay*, Canto 6: Fire of the Archer, p.72.

[24] *DoorWay*, Canto 6: Fire of the Archer, p. 80 and then similarly on pp. 85 and 86.

After a while of travelling on an eagle's back, visiting poets and places sublime, it is as if the son's work of helping to reconcile his father with his history is done and so the child 'broke

> Away, resumed that from I'd followed. Now
> A butterfly, disappearing as smoke'[25].

But then suddenly, 'Butterfly Appeared[26]' to take his father on a final flight – both through a portrayal of the end times and to wake, finally, in the bed beside which his 'lovely Linda's sitting',

> Holding my hand, awaiting God's great plan
> To bring me back to life, and let me sing
>
> Of plot – His plot – where all of it began:
> The love of God for woman and for man'[27].

So, in contrast to the violence of an abortion and what it does to the child, the mother and the father,

---

[25] *DoorWay*, Canto 6: Fire of the Archer, p. 86.

[26] *DoorWay*, Canto 8: Love in Canis Major, p. 115.

[27] *DoorWay*, Canto 9: Arriving in Aquarius, p. 134.

there is this image of the butterfly which almost seems to manifest, albeit in an accelerated way, the passage from conception to manhood – through the embrace of a reconciling forgiveness. Nevertheless, retaining the image of the butterfly reminds us, poignantly, of the real beauty and fragility of the gift of the person: that there was a time when the child was not – even if he ever was in the foresight of God before being begotten. But, after conception, there is now never a time when that child is not; for, just as who comes to exist, comes to exist for ever more, so fatherhood and motherhood are inseparably, and enduringly, forevermore.

In a wonderful way, then, the butterfly expresses both the fleeting, flimsiness of a human life, but even more the power of One who can hold in existence what would otherwise have been obliterated. But God more than holds in existence, a brief life; rather, He enables that brief life to be lived more fully than ordinarily it would be possible to do so. We are left, then, with more than a symbol of the victory of love over death – of Christ over sin – that both permeates the father-son relationship and, through it, expresses that Fatherhood of God. We are left with a tangible love which God untangled from the suffering in which it existed, to reveal that the life which God had created is ever called to love and to be loved by the God who loves all.

The freedom of the butterfly emphasizes, too, the freedom to seek God and, like a homing pigeon, to draw others to Him. By contrast, the image we began with in *HellWard* becomes even more forceful and, in the light of the butterfly, has a certain mirroring about it. Thus, the children, which seem alive in the wall of the man who abused his sexuality, are more a symbol of the unfulfilled, tormented manhood of the man himself, rather than a doomed judgement of the children themselves. So, the contrasting imagery is not just about the difference between the reality of a frustrated and a fulfilling fatherhood; but, too, entails a hope that in the mercy of God there is a living presence of all who were untimely dead. Or, as in the case of the author and his aborted child, were ensnared in suffocating sufferings – both literally and psychologically. And, simultaneously, the power of prayer is discovered to be a source of surprise to all who pray and do not know how God will answer – But God will answer.

In Conclusion

I am very conscious that my response to James Sale's work is not in terms of its poetic significance except in so far as his imagery has had a powerful effect on me. Nevertheless, in that he addresses the beginning and end of life, literally, and that his vision spreads out, as it were, like light through a breach, it seems appropriate to consider his overarching theme: from personal suffering and tragedy to the all encompassing vision of God for the good of all – even if, although we do not know for certain, that all human beings will accept it. But, again, even within that progressively widening scope, including as it does all kinds of relationships, and whether or not those relationships can be reconciled in terms of truth and love, there is the one I have singled out: that of father and aborted son.

This both deserves attention in its own right and because it is scarcely addressed in our society. In reality, if we take into account all the different ways that sex is exploited, denatured, abused, there are probably more fatherless children than can ever be counted – except in the awakened conscience of each man.

Therefore, to single out what is seen, or rather witnessed in this poetic expression of a fatherless fathering of children, because the author has traversed the fuller reality of a child lost and found in the presence of God, makes it all the more urgent to cry out about the pain and joy the loss and finding a child entails. But in order to share the pain and joy the man has had to pass through that terrible and tortuous self-examination that only goes to show how profoundly deeply, deeper than a passing fathering, is the real reality of fatherhood.

In sum, while there is not exactly a sequence of events that runs, as I have run it, yet the squashing and wasting of fatherhood does permeate this trilogy of Sale's and, while it takes up his own personal experience, he "confesses" the fault of many – if not many more than we will ever know, and acts as an agent of conversion: of turning us to both the what men are really like and what promise, in fact, the embodied expression of fatherhood promises for fulfilment of men.

This work, then, in the great tradition of Christian confessional works, serves both art and the healing of hearts. I invite you to read it in the light of your own, actual life, and let it scour what is imperfect and perfect what is the present: the original gift of God: 'The love of God for woman and for man'.

What follows is an account of my own experience of a child lost to abortion.

INDELIBLE: AN UNEXPECTED JOY: AN UNPRECEDENTED PAIN[28]

Sin does not describe the experience of suddenly, unexpectedly, discovering an inexplicable joy that arises out of the conception of a child; indeed, however aware we were of the possibility of conceiving a child, there came an unforgettable joy from the very roots of human being. Whatever the "noisy" claims about a "clump of cells" - the reality of parenthood had an unmistakable beginning: a trumpeting joy. It is possible to understand human psychology as if our whole being is a kind of self-originating expression of conscious reactions; however, given that the very existence of each one of us arises out of relationships, it is not possible to understand ourselves except "through" relationship. Perhaps we need to recog-

---

[28] From the book, *The Prayerful Kiss*.

nise, then, that seeing is seeing something or someone: that there is a kind of interior dialogue between ourselves and what exists. Consciousness is not just about "admitting" the presence of a self – it is also about dialoguing with what is real. Thus, on reflection, the joy that arose was as indistinguishable from the very coming into existence of "another" as it was unbidden; indeed, as surrounded as this moment was by all kinds of difficulties and uncertainties, it is extraordinary that it was joy that rang out.

Joy and pain express "relationship"

But then the child was aborted. Whatever was half-thought about the existence of a beginning, an initial moment of animation, the various possibilities of our lives, the pain of discovering that that child's life had been abruptly, terribly ended, was a pain as uninvited and prolonged as the joy had been brief and brilliant. Thirty years on, however, this child is as present to me as every other child; and, even if I cannot explain it, I am conscious of a fatherhood that I cannot forget. Just as children are constantly around me, as I am now married and my wife and I have ten children, two of whom miscarried and we hope are also in heaven, so this child of thirty years ago is as present to me as they all are. Even if one is away from the dining room table, whether just briefly for a party elsewhere, an outing or for a longer expedition, it is not possible to describe, adequately, the "silence" of the children's absence. Thus, this child of thirty years is still present in "his" absence in a way that makes a lie of every account that denies the reality of both the unborn and the relationship which comes into existence with the very beginning of each child.

Recognising an unborn child is about recognizing the "reality" of relationship

Whether a child is lost through a miscarriage or an abortion, never mind the many other possibilities that can bring about such a loss, there is an inseparable relationship which has come to exist and which continues, unabated, to call for development; indeed, as difficult as it is to understand, a relationship can undergo all kinds of changes even through the mystery of death. To begin with, there is seeking forgiveness and asking for help; indeed, Charlie's abortion, while an indelible experience, did not of itself make me chaste. The pain, however, made me conscious of another relationship: the relationship of mother and child – the relationship of the Mother of God and her son Jesus Christ. As what Mother Teresa would call a 'broken Christian', I vacillated between going to Church and living a life that expressed an inability to commit myself to anyone or anything. Nevertheless, in that "moment" of grief, I was vividly conscious of the dead Christ in the arms of His Mother; and, at the same time, the unavoidable consciousness of the painful death of the innocent: the innocence of Christ and the innocence of Charlie. If it can be called a consolation – although it is scarcely possible to experience the comfort of that consolation, so painful is the realisation of participation, however inadvertent and unintended, in the event of abortion – then it was as if the Mother of the Lord communicated the mystery of salvation: that just as the death of her own Son was not in vain, neither was the death of this child in vain. Indeed, if the loss of one child can cause so much pain, how much unacknowledged suffering must exist because of the daily denial of human fatherhood?

What about, too, the discovery that anyone who has "given" a part of what constitutes the mystery of life to another or to an experiment has given a relationship of life to life, of one person to another, that is as real as the living being that has come into existence? We live in a culture, then, that at some time will discover – or become more dreadful in its denial – that we live amidst a multitude of relationships that it may take our entry into eternity to actually admit, acknowledge and address as the real effect of our actions.

Religious experience and pain are not conversion

Pain discloses all kinds of regret and impoverishment, from an uncertainty about vocation, abilities and training to the intricate, difficult and challenging depths that are at work in our lives. In other words, even if these experiences began to make it clear that I could not marry because I did not have faith, they neither made it clear what faith was nor how to come to it; indeed, I can remember thinking that I could not marry because I did not have the faith to endure the inescapable sufferings of marriage – yet I could not have told you what it was about faith that made it possible to endure the sufferings of marriage. Clearly, however, there was some nascent awareness that faith makes possible endurance. Thus, by default, as it were, I discovered that I neither had faith nor knew what it was. But, at the same time as my life showed more and more clearly the devastation wrought from within, I was almost involuntarily incapable of finding truth to be a sufficient answer to the disorder which was increasingly evident. I could recognise, for example, that for years I had been seeking to find a path to employment: a path which both identified a particular, "workable talent" and, at the same time, the number of different routes that I chose to pursue argued, cumulatively, for the realisation that I did not know who I was. I did not seem to possess a stable identity. I was neither married nor single, neither priest nor monk, neither writer nor painter, neither sculptor nor craftsman, although I had "passed through" the possibility of being all of them and had ended up as none of them.

Self-discovery is not the same as being discovered by God

Certain insights are, as it were, like the rediscovery of the human being: that each human person is essentially relational: that the human person is constituted by origin, relationship and identity: that each person is both an originator and a recipient of relationships. But we originate relationships, not because we brought ourselves into existence, but because we were "caused" to exist: we were loved into existence. Love, in a sense, is nothing if not relational; it is impossible to love if there is no one to love. The point, then, of this is that there are many invaluable insights about the heart of human personhood which arise, incidentally, in the course of truly seeking to bring about a whole human existence: an answer to the pain of not knowing exactly who we are and the purpose of life.

Not only, then, is relationship the dynamic vehicle of self-development; but, in a sense, the refusal of relationship is at the root of psychological problems. I recall, for instance, being unable and indeed "unwilling" to admit the pain of humiliations that I experienced as a school child; and, as a result, I "throttled" the whole, human reaction, which would have disclosed the interior of my childhood. It was not until much later, then, that I rediscovered the experience that had once been a part of my "present". The "living memory" had "remained" but had been inaccessible until a "dam" broke and I became conscious of streaming memories, unabated, as if like compost it cannot become a part of the ground out of which comes growth until it has more naturally "soaked" in and through consciousness. The thought, then, that arises from the material of our experience, needs that experience to be available in the kind of way that voluntary recall makes possible; but if, for whatever reason, pride speaks through the unwillingness to admit sufferings, then not only does pride itself remain hidden but so, too, do the dynamics of development which depend on self-disclosure.

The recovery of personal history, however, is not the same as recognising the history of salvation; and, while philosophical naturalism has immense merits, it is not the same as discovering ourselves in the action of God. Thus, discovering our foundational relationship to God is essential, not just to the truth of life but to conversion: that just as God created all that exists from nothing so He can make a new beginning for the sinner (cf. *Catechism of the Catholic Church*, paragraph 298). In the prose-poem which follows there is a brief account of the pain and joy of becoming a father and then losing the child to abortion.

INDELIBLE

Joy announced you to me.

I know the smothering imperfection of our time:
the anxious lying of single people –
am I a father? am I a mother?
do we have a child?

"Your" existence your mother denied:
her lie to my uncertainty, a slipperiness supplied –
and my heart filled,
as I foresaw her,
beside me,

stretching out our tent:
swelling,
growing rounder
and my hands and body knowing
life between us growing
from within us both beginning
but now in her becoming –

And again I pulled apart:

"Are we married?
Have we the right?
To love as lovers and unite?"

But then I saw, as in a sleepless dream,
in an in-hospitable place, being done what we cannot undo:

separating what God had joined together.

Chapter Three : «DoorWay» to «The Lord of All»

Your mother and I met again,
and her secret, she shared:

That she thought you were a "blobby mass";
and, because of it,

You are no longer where you were.

*Listening was a splashing pain,
a splintering, swiftly slicing pain.*

"I'm sorry" was a word too heavily burdened to be spoken.

We named and prayed for you.

Too personal, I know, to make public, but public it now is,
because too many died, before you,
and you did to me what millions did not do.

I was wrong, I know, to love when love was not committed, between your mother and me.

Listening was a splashing pain,
a splintering, swiftly lashing pain.

And I pulled apart again - hurting hard again:

a hidden shard of pain,
seizing leaving as a means
to hurt her hard again.

.

"I am sorry": a word that grew in me to speak.

Listening was a splashing pain,
a splintering, swiftly swiping pain.

"I am sorry" is a word to strengthen the weak.

Reconciled
Your mother and I parted.

The dead Christ-child lay in the arms of Mary:
a blooming brightening
unforgettable being.
And out of Love's many-chambered-petalled-heart,
our child spoke like scent:

> "Look and see the Crucified:
> His Resurrection is our new life.
> Do not escape your suffering and
> it will give you life again.
>
> When Easter crowns the crucifixion and
> completes the gift of Christmas –
> we will go up in song,
> and love will cry out:
> Amen in song!
> Amen in sight!
> Amen!

Conclusion

His Judgement is Mercy

While I do not remember exactly what prompted the following thought, I do remember discussing three of the last things with a priest with whom I once worked. Thus, one of my earliest thoughts on the three last things is that of there being three responses to the fire of love: the fire of love is a torment to those who do not want to be loved; the fire of love purifies and cleanses the heart of its hardness, as it were, opening the heart to the fullest extent of a person's willingness to love; and the fire of love that fills and intoxicates, owing to the abundant presence of the love of God that is poured into our hearts (cf. Romans 5: 5).

Thoughts of death and judgment may have roots in our lives and we may not admit them or they may emerge to be developed. I remember, particularly, trying to take my life at about 14. Why I did not succeed was because I had a kind of vision of being judged by Christ and His disciples and so I started drinking water and, as is evident, I lived to tell of what happened nearly 56 years, eleven children of my own, and over twenty books ago. In other words the fear of God, which Scripture calls the beginning of wisdom (cf. Proverbs 9: 10), was what moved me to live; and, even if living was for many years an impossible experience, the grace of God has triumphed more and more over my inability to believe that God loves me and wants the fullness of life promised in His word: "I come to give you life and life to the full" (John 10: 10).

Inevitably, then, we come to this work on the three last things with various thoughts and experiences of our own. Nevertheless, even if there are many lacunae and "holes", as it were, in an account of *HellWard's Hell*, *StairWell's Purgatory*, and *DoorWay's Heaven* and, in addition, there remain many aspects of this epic trilogy of James Sale's which remain unexplored. Nevertheless, his work engages us with the questions which need to be addressed. Thus, the two themes that have particularly emerged are "relationship" and the "power of imagery" to communicate to conscience the call to look at our lives as we actually live, realizing that we are all approaching the great, irreversible, final moment of death. Distinguishing, then, between those warning events of illness and tragedy, and the path of life which leads through death, helping us to live in the light of death's opening upon eternity.

So, it is indeed absolutely necessary to confront the possibility of death, and not to be defeated at the outset. There are people to whom the subject of death is impossible to countenance; and, therefore, when death takes a husband, wife, child or friend, they are devastated and unable, sometimes, either to rally or to live on in the light of this event. Thus, we need writers, like James Sale, to remind us to consider our experience of life and the relationships which Christ needs to heal and to help if we are to enter eternal life – either at all or ready to recognize that our welcome depends on our welcome of others. In other words, even if there are many reason why we were hurt or hurt others, yet there is only one reason why prayer becomes the Christian – and that is because Christ prayed, in the midst of the unutterable torment of the crucifixion, "Father, forgive them for they know not what they do" (Luke 23: 34).

Thus, the final judgement is: be merciful to others in the hope of obtaining mercy ourselves.

www.ingramcontent.com/pod-product-compliance
Lightning Source LLC
Chambersburg PA
CBHW070853050426
42453CB00012B/2183